FALL

FALL

Ron Hirschi

Photographs by
Thomas D. Mangelsen

A WILDLIFE SEASONS BOOK

Cobblehill Books
Dutton • New York

Library of Congress Cataloging-in-Publication Data

Hirschi, Ron.
    Fall / Ron Hirschi ; photographs by Thomas D. Mangelsen.
        p.   cm.
    "A Wildlife seasons book."
    Summary: Introduces the characteristics of autumn in simple
text and illustrations.
    ISBN 0-525-65053-9
    1. Autumn—Juvenile literature.   2. Nature study—Juvenile
literature.   [1. Autumn.]   I. Mangelsen, Thomas D., ill.
II. Title.
QH81.H653   1991
508—dc20   90-19595
                                                                  CIP
                                                                   AC

Published in the United States by Cobblehill Books,
an affiliate of Dutton Children's Books,
a division of Penguin Books USA Inc.

Designer: Charlotte Staub
Printed in Hong Kong   First edition
10 9 8 7 6 5 4 3 2 1

To the Kids of
Columbus   R.H.

For my mother,
Margaret Berenice,
who has given so much
to her children   T.M.

Tips of trees with
red and golden leaves
will tell you.
The sound of geese
will too.
Long days of summer
are over.

The first round moon of fall is here.

The last flower petals fall as seeds from lilies, larkspurs, and shooting stars drop to the ground.

Now the spiders spin strong webs.

Red squirrel

Hickory nuts, acorns, and conifer cones fall to the ground and squirrels harvest each tree's treasure.

Gray jay

In the crunch of leaves beneath the trees, wild turkeys search for acorns. Jays hide most of what they find.

Wild turkey

Cliff swallows

Fall is time for the swallow flocks to gather.
Quick as the wind, the summer birds disappear.
They fly to southern lands, to a southern spring.

Barn swallows

September sun ripens red berries—the sweet fruit is plucked by coyotes, cardinals, and woodpeckers too.

Cardinal

Soapberries

Deep in the woods, the oldest trees bend in autumn winds. Great-grandparents of the forest, a hundred years and more of leaves have fallen from each ancient tree.

Now, mushrooms sprout in their deep, rich soil for deer to chew, for squirrels to nibble.

Red squirrel

Mule deer

When strong winds pull the leaves from the highest branches, sometimes an old tree will fall. Laying on the ground, the tree is still a welcome home where rabbits, raccoons, or foxes hide.

Red fox

Raccoon

Sockeye salmon

Out near the Pacific Ocean coast, salmon swim in from the sea. They return to the river of their birth, instinctively. Salmon lay their eggs in clean river gravel.

Then, the parent fish all die.

Fall is time for the eagles to return to the salmon rivers. They know when the fish will appear. The majestic birds swoop down to feast on salmon while the river slips endlessly back out to sea.

Bald eagle

Sandhill cranes

Cold nights and frosty mornings, then a dust of snow appears. Geese and cranes and tiny bluebirds too — they all turn south in family flocks.

They know
winter is
near.

AFTERWORD

Fall days turn cooler and nights longer. It is a season of rapid transformation. The birth of spring and growth of summer are tested now, as animals prepare for the winter ahead. Birds that hatched only a few months earlier must be strong enough to fly hundreds, sometimes thousands of miles. Bears and other hibernators must eat enough so their body fat will last through the cold months of winter.

Fall is also a time for dramatic events that remind us how life is connected to endless natural cycles. In coastal rivers, adult salmon return to the place of birth after having spent two or more years in the ocean. The salmon die after spawning, but their bodies give new life to eagles, bears, coyotes, river otters, raccoons, weasels, bobcats, gulls, and many more animals. Plants along the riverbanks are also enriched by nutrients brought to land by the seagoing salmon.

The few ancient forests that still remain untouched by axes and saws offer one of the most wonderful views of the cycle from death to new life. Decaying wood from fallen trees enriches deep soil layers that support new generations of trees. The ground of the old forests are carpeted with dense layers of moss and a complex covering of ferns, mushrooms, orchids, and more. No matter where plants grow, this same natural cycle occurs each fall—as death comes to a leaf, a branch, or an entire plant other forms of life spring from the remains. It is as if the earth is fattening itself each fall, consuming fallen leaves in preparation for a long winter sleep.